Branding Your Brilliance

A Step-by-Step Guide
to Personal Branding

Dr. Catherine Epps

Branding Your Brilliance

Copyright© 2023 Catherine Epps

For permissions requests, write to the publisher at the address below:
info@apalmettopharmacist.net

ISBN: 979-8-9882543-3-1

Disclaimer

The information contained in this book is for general informational purposes only. While the author and publisher have made every effort to ensure that the information provided in this book is accurate and up to date, they make no representations or warranties of any kind, express or implied, about the completeness, accuracy, reliability, suitability, or availability concerning the book or the information, products, services, or related graphics contained in the book for any purpose.

In no event will the author or publisher be liable for any loss or damage, including, without limitation, indirect or consequential loss or damage, or any loss or damage whatsoever arising from loss of data or profits arising out of, or in connection with, the use of this book. Every effort has been made to accurately represent people, places, events, or facts mentioned in this book. However, any resemblance to actual persons, living or dead, or actual events is purely coincidental.

The views and opinions expressed in this book are solely those of the author and do not necessarily reflect the official policy or position of any other individual, agency, organization, or company. If you have any concerns or questions about the content of this book, please consult a qualified professional in the relevant field.

Please note that this book may contain references to websites, resources, or services that are not controlled by the author or publisher. These references are provided for informational purposes only and do not imply endorsement or recommendation of any kind.

About the Author

Dr. Catherine Epps is a graduate of Virginia Commonwealth University with a Doctor of Pharmacy degree. She has spent over 20 years hiring hundreds of amazing professionals, conducting thousands of interviews, and reviewing tens of thousands of resumes in leadership positions: hiring, training, mentoring, and developing individuals throughout their careers.

Now Dr. Epps pursues a fulfilling career; mentoring, coaching, authoring, and advising, passing on her tips and secrets to stand out in a crowded field to be considered the expert in your field, influencer, and highly sought-after for career advancement. She has written books on personal branding, career transition, video courses covering branding and career development, and provides individual career coaching sessions.

She hopes you will find her experiences, education, tips, and tricks helpful to your journey. If you head to her website, apalmettopharmacist.com, you will find a free tip sheet with pages of branding examples.

Feel free to email at apalmettopharmacist@gmail.com, subject line, "community," to join the professional community for monthly advice, offers, and exclusive tips.

Preface

Many people cringe when they hear the phrase "personal branding." But in today's world, personal branding has become an essential aspect of our lives. Whether you are an entrepreneur, a job seeker, or a new or established professional, building a personal brand is crucial to your success. However, personal branding can be vague and confusing, leaving many people unsure how to approach it.

I understand the challenges of building a personal brand. When I was starting my business, I found explanations of branding were often too abstract or not applicable to my situation. I struggled to find actionable steps that I could take to build my brand. I wrote this book to provide a comprehensive guide to personal branding that is practical, actionable, and easy to understand and share personal experiences and insights on how to build a solid personal brand that will help you achieve your goals.

The book is divided into three parts. Part one focuses on understanding personal branding, such as defining your brand, identifying your target audience, creating a brand strategy, choosing your messaging platforms, and analyzing results.

Part two is all about building your brand. It provides practical tips on creating a brand identity, developing a brand voice, establishing a brand presence online and offline, and strategies for growth.

Part three is about leveraging your brand to achieve your goals. It covers networking, building relationships, and creating a personal brand that brilliantly outshines the rest.

Table of Contents

Chapter One

―――――∧―――――

Branding For the Win

A CEO is wrestling with the decision of whom to hire for the VP position that has just opened in their organization. The talent pool of candidates has been narrowed to two standout applicants. Both applicants are equally qualified, and judging from their respective resumes, each would do a stellar job. The CEO faces a decisive question: which one gets the job?

To aid in their decision, the CEO looks at the social media of both applicants, much like 90–98% of potential employers (according to small biz trenz).

Applicant A has a LinkedIn profile page that was last updated five years ago. Their Instagram page publicly displays photos that show fun but possibly embarrassing moments, and their Twitter profile shows highly charged tweet debates.

On the other hand, Applicant B has developed a personal brand demonstrated on social media that contains thoughtful discussions on industry topics, updated professional social platforms with current, relevant content, fun and candid content on Facebook; their Instagram is discreetly private; their network has been cultivated so that the CEO not only recognizes several followers, but some mutual connections have contacted them on behalf of Applicant B.

Applicant B will likely tip the scales and win the VP position. The small amount of time and effort taken by Applicant B to develop a personal brand would pay off. The CEO of a company would take comfort in the care, effort, and professionalism Applicant B has taken concerning their professional image. Therefore, the CEO can entrust their company's brand with Applicant B.

Chapter Two

Creating Your Brand

What Personal Branding Is Not

It is inevitable that everyone you encounter in your professional and personal life will develop an opinion of you. Not only that, but they will make a superficial judgment concerning what kind of professional you are.

But you are in control of cultivating your brand with your vision.

Personal branding is not about logos, color schemes, or slogans. It's about expressing your identity by shaping the narrative to display your professional expertise, bringing visibility to yourself, and establishing credibility.

Personal branding is not about "fake it 'till you make it. This is terrible advice. Why? Because people see through fakeness and are insulted by something that resembles trickery.

If you are not where you would like to be professional, avoid trying to be somebody you're not; the best path is to be authentic with your journey and share your experience, knowledge, growth, and continued goals.

What Personal Branding is

Personal branding is about gaining clarity about the role you want in life, what you want to be known for, how you want to be remembered, and the goals you want to achieve.

Branding is about controlling the narrative so others see your talents, skills, ambitions, interests, and professionalism instead of making inferences from random information they access about you, whether through observation or checking your social media.

Personal branding is also about creating a clear message that concisely describes all the above, which can be shared through social media, resumes, profiles, and an introduction when you are announced as a speaker or introduced at a networking event.

Suppose you walk up to a group of people mingling in casual conversation with an acquaintance who can quickly introduce you and describe you naturally and professionally. In that case, you have successfully created your brand.

This is because your brand has established a comfort level that gives others trust in your authority as a specialist and expert in your field. It also makes you a genuinely likable person people want to get to know.

The more you are your authentic self, the more it resonates with others and draws them in. The goal is for future employers, your industry, colleagues, and those in your sphere who see your personal brand to be attracted and want more, to be drawn in and part of your culture.

Components of Your Personal Brand

So, now that you know what a personal brand is, how do you create one? Understand that it consists of four components.

To develop your brand, you will have to:

Construct a Personal Value Statement — An elevator pitch is the central theme of your brand.

Design Messaging — Through social media profiles, resume and cover letter, development, and speaker introduction, you will populate your social media platforms with professional and relevant materials.

Cultivate a Network — By recognizing the power of your network, you will curate, support, and lean into the power of that network.

Control the Message — Consistently reinforce your brand, advance the strength of your authority, nurture your network, and creatively increase your brand awareness.

You are already a brand, so let it be you who demonstrate your talents, skills, experiences, vision, and goals in an authentic voice and positively shape your message.

Chapter Three

Personal Purpose Statement

A Statement of Many Names

Your personal purpose statement is also called your "value-added statement." It could also be called your "mission statement," your "personal value statement," or your "personal vision statement."

The core components of a personal purpose statement are your values, beliefs, goals, purpose, mission, talents, skills, abilities, and dreams. These are what make you unique and different from everybody else.

They should reflect who you are, what you offer, and where you are going. It should be concise and, most importantly, not sound generic or robotic but ring with your authentic voice.

Elevator Pitch vs. What Mom Would Say

Once you have defined your personal purpose statement, it will make networking easier when asked, "And what do you do?" It means you will never have writer's block again when someone asks you to submit a bio for the company website or to conduct a speaker's introduction.

Some people call this your "elevator pitch" because you should be able to know it so well you can recite it at a moment's notice (such as the duration of an elevator ride); it should pique someone's interest and get key points across in a brief amount of time.

I define a remarkable personal brand statement like this. When someone asks your mom what you do, instead of giving a vague (and uninspiring) answer like, "He's a personal trainer," she instead responds, "He is a certified personal trainer specialized in keeping professional athletes in top shape."

If mom can deliver that description while playing pickleball, then, my friend, you have crafted your brand statement well.

Key Element of Personal Purpose Statement

The main segments of the statement will contain your talents and skills, your niche audience, your goals and aspirations, and what makes you different from the rest.

Values

Let's talk about values. What are some traits you value?

Values you connect with should be considered when writing your personal statement.

You may be empathetic, a good listener, optimistic, curious, a life learner, patient, or called into servant leadership.

As an exercise, write down the traits, talents, and values that describe you, then underline what you consider to be your most important traits.

Skills and Experience

Next, what are your skills and experiences? These are learned through trade, apprenticeship, college, graduate school, internships, and work experience. But also consider volunteer work, mentorship, and life experience.

Maybe you are passionate about leadership, mentorship, clinical research, or improving patients' lives. Or you crush sales goals, drive operational efficiencies, build relationships, or engage audiences.

Personal Value Statement Blueprint:

Step One:

"I am ___ (what you do, blended with education and certification)

Step Two:

With ___ (values and unique aspects to you),

Step Three:

Looking to do ___ (goals and aspirations)."

Use powerful words to compel the reader:

Power words: facilitated, led, constructed, built, reduced, enhanced, engaged.

Less powerful words: provided, made sure, performed, participated.

Example Value Statement:

"Passionate to serve the most vulnerable seniors by providing clinical resources to improve their quality of life through safe and innovative pharmaceutical care."

"Passionate to serve the most vulnerable seniors by providing clinical resources to improve their quality of life through safe and innovative pharmaceutical care."

Step One:

"I am _ _ _ an expert with clinical resources and pharmaceutical care (what you do, blended with education and certification).

Step Two:

With_ _ _ a passion for serving a vulnerable population (your talent is your innovative and compassionate values and particular aspects)

Step Three:

I am looking to do_ _ _ to improve senior's quality of life" (goals and aspirations).

EXAMPLE BREAKDOWN

NURSING

"DELIVERING COMPASSIONATE AND PATIENT-CENTERED CARE TO PROMOTE OPTIMAL HEALTH OUTCOMES."

"UTILIZING A MULTIDISCIPLINARY APPROACH TO CARE DELIVERY THAT EMPHASIZES COLLABORATION, COMMUNICATION, AND TEAMWORK."

"STAYING UP-TO-DATE WITH THE LATEST RESEARCH, TECHNOLOGIES, AND BEST PRACTICES IN NURSING TO ENSURE EVIDENCE-BASED CARE."

"DEMONSTRATING A STRONG WORK ETHIC AND COMMITMENT TO PROVIDING EXCEPTIONAL CARE TO PATIENTS AND FAMILIES."

"PROVIDING EMOTIONAL SUPPORT AND COUNSELING TO PATIENTS AND FAMILIES TO ADDRESS PSYCHOSOCIAL NEEDS."

"EMPHASIZING THE IMPORTANCE OF HEALTH PROMOTION, DISEASE PREVENTION, AND HEALTH EDUCATION IN NURSING PRACTICE."

"UTILIZING A HOLISTIC APPROACH TO CARE THAT ADDRESSES PHYSICAL, EMOTIONAL, AND SPIRITUAL NEEDS OF PATIENTS."

"PROVIDING ADVOCACY AND SUPPORT FOR PATIENTS WITH CHRONIC ILLNESSES AND DISABILITIES."

"BUILDING STRONG RELATIONSHIPS WITH HEALTHCARE PROVIDERS, COMMUNITY ORGANIZATIONS, AND OTHER STAKEHOLDERS TO ENSURE COORDINATED AND EFFECTIVE CARE DELIVERY."

EXAMPLE BREAKDOWN

MARKETING

"BUILDING AND EXECUTING STRATEGIC MARKETING PLANS THAT DRIVE BRAND AWARENESS, ENGAGEMENT, AND REVENUE GROWTH."

"PROVIDING EXPERT KNOWLEDGE OF MARKET TRENDS, CUSTOMER BEHAVIOR, AND EMERGING TECHNOLOGIES TO INFORM MARKETING STRATEGIES."

"UTILIZING DATA-DRIVEN INSIGHTS TO MEASURE AND OPTIMIZE CAMPAIGN PERFORMANCE AND ENSURE MAXIMUM ROI."

"UTILIZING DIGITAL MARKETING CHANNELS AND TECHNOLOGIES TO REACH AND ENGAGE TARGET AUDIENCES ACROSS VARIOUS PLATFORMS."

"DELIVERING CLEAR AND TRANSPARENT COMMUNICATION TO CLIENTS TO ENSURE THEY ARE WELL INFORMED THROUGHOUT THE MARKETING PROCESS."

"EMPHASIZING THE IMPORTANCE OF CUSTOMER-CENTRIC MARKETING STRATEGIES TO BUILD BRAND LOYALTY AND ADVOCACY."

"STAYING UP-TO-DATE WITH THE LATEST MARKETING TRENDS, TECHNOLOGIES, AND BEST PRACTICES TO STAY AHEAD OF THE COMPETITION."

"DEVELOPING AND EXECUTING SUCCESSFUL EVENT MARKETING STRATEGIES TO INCREASE BRAND EXPOSURE AND DRIVE CUSTOMER ENGAGEMENT."

"DEMONSTRATING A COMMITMENT TO ONGOING LEARNING AND PROFESSIONAL DEVELOPMENT TO STAY AHEAD OF INDUSTRY TRENDS AND BEST PRACTICES."

EXAMPLE BREAKDOWN

INVESTMENT BANKING

"PROVIDING EXPERT KNOWLEDGE AND ADVICE TO CLIENTS ON COMPLEX FINANCIAL TRANSACTIONS AND INVESTMENT STRATEGIES."

"UTILIZING DEEP KNOWLEDGE OF MARKETS, INDUSTRIES, AND INVESTMENT TRENDS TO IDENTIFY AND EXECUTE HIGH-VALUE OPPORTUNITIES FOR CLIENTS."

"PROVIDING COMPREHENSIVE FINANCIAL ANALYSIS AND MODELING TO INFORM INVESTMENT DECISIONS AND IDENTIFY POTENTIAL RISKS."

"EMPHASIZING THE IMPORTANCE OF MARKET RESEARCH AND DATA-DRIVEN DECISION-MAKING TO ENSURE SUCCESS IN INVESTMENT STRATEGIES."

"PROVIDING GUIDANCE AND SUPPORT TO CLIENTS TO HELP THEM NAVIGATE COMPLEX FINANCIAL TRANSACTIONS."

"STAYING UP-TO-DATE WITH LEGAL AND REGULATORY CHANGES THAT IMPACT THE INVESTMENT INDUSTRY."

"DEMONSTRATING A COMMITMENT TO ONGOING LEARNING AND PROFESSIONAL DEVELOPMENT TO STAY AHEAD OF INDUSTRY TRENDS AND BEST PRACTICES."

"PROVIDING THOUGHT LEADERSHIP IN THE INDUSTRY THROUGH PUBLISHING AND SPEAKING ENGAGEMENTS."

"BUILDING A STRONG BRAND REPUTATION AND DELIVERING A CONSISTENT AND EXCEPTIONAL CLIENT EXPERIENCE TO SUPPORT BUSINESS GROWTH."

EXAMPLE BREAKDOWN

REAL ESTATE AGENT

"PROVIDING EXPERT KNOWLEDGE OF LOCAL REAL ESTATE MARKETS, TRENDS, AND PROPERTY VALUES TO HELP CLIENTS MAKE INFORMED DECISIONS."

"STAYING UP-TO-DATE WITH THE LATEST TECHNOLOGIES AND TOOLS TO ENSURE A SEAMLESS AND EFFICIENT BUYING OR SELLING PROCESS FOR CLIENTS."

"PROVIDING A FULL-SERVICE APPROACH TO REAL ESTATE TRANSACTIONS, INCLUDING STAGING, PHOTOGRAPHY, AND LEGAL SUPPORT."

"EMPHASIZING THE IMPORTANCE OF MARKET RESEARCH AND DATA-DRIVEN DECISION-MAKING TO ENSURE SUCCESS IN BUYING OR SELLING PROPERTIES."

"PROVIDING CONTINUOUS COMMUNICATION AND SUPPORT THROUGHOUT THE ENTIRE REAL ESTATE PROCESS."

"BUILDING A STRONG BRAND REPUTATION AND DELIVERING A CONSISTENT AND EXCEPTIONAL CLIENT EXPERIENCE TO SUPPORT REAL ESTATE GROWTH."

EXAMPLE
BREAKDOWN

EDUCATORS

"EMPOWERING STUDENTS TO BECOME LIFELONG LEARNERS THROUGH ENGAGING AND INTERACTIVE TEACHING METHODS."

"CREATING A SAFE AND INCLUSIVE CLASSROOM ENVIRONMENT WHERE ALL STUDENTS CAN THRIVE AND ACHIEVE THEIR POTENTIAL."

"CULTIVATING A GROWTH MINDSET IN STUDENTS BY FOSTERING A LOVE OF LEARNING AND ENCOURAGING RISK-TAKING."

"DEDICATED TO PROVIDING PERSONALIZED AND DIFFERENTIATED INSTRUCTION TO MEET THE UNIQUE NEEDS OF EACH STUDENT."

"HELPING STUDENTS DEVELOP STRONG COMMUNICATION AND COLLABORATION SKILLS TO PREPARE THEM FOR SUCCESS IN THE FUTURE."

"ENCOURAGING A LOVE OF READING AND LITERATURE BY INCORPORATING DIVERSE AND CULTURALLY RELEVANT TEXTS INTO THE CURRICULUM."

"PASSIONATE ABOUT PROMOTING CREATIVITY AND SELF-EXPRESSION IN STUDENTS THROUGH ART, MUSIC, AND OTHER MEDIUMS."

"COMMITTED TO FOSTERING A LOVE OF STEM SUBJECTS AND PREPARING STUDENTS FOR CAREERS IN SCIENCE, TECHNOLOGY, ENGINEERING, AND MATH."

"PRIORITIZING SOCIAL AND EMOTIONAL LEARNING TO SUPPORT STUDENTS' OVERALL WELL-BEING AND DEVELOPMENT."

EXAMPLE BREAKDOWN

SALES POSITIONS

"LEADING HIGH-PERFORMANCE SALES TEAMS THAT CONSISTENTLY EXCEED TARGETS AND DRIVE REVENUE GROWTH."

"FOSTERING A CULTURE OF COLLABORATION AND ACCOUNTABILITY TO ENSURE THE SUCCESSFUL EXECUTION OF SALES STRATEGIES."

"DEVELOPING AND IMPLEMENTING INNOVATIVE SALES STRATEGIES THAT ADAPT TO CHANGING MARKET CONDITIONS AND CUSTOMER NEEDS."

"BUILDING AND NURTURING A TALENT PIPELINE TO ATTRACT AND RETAIN TOP SALES TALENT IN THE INDUSTRY."

"DEMONSTRATING A DEEP UNDERSTANDING OF MARKET TRENDS, COMPETITIVE LANDSCAPES, AND EMERGING OPPORTUNITIES."

"UTILIZING DATA-DRIVEN INSIGHTS TO INFORM STRATEGIC DECISION-MAKING AND OPTIMIZE SALES PERFORMANCE."

"CULTIVATING A STRONG NETWORK OF INDUSTRY CONNECTIONS TO FACILITATE STRATEGIC PARTNERSHIPS AND BUSINESS OPPORTUNITIES."

"EMPOWERING SALES TEAMS TO TAKE OWNERSHIP OF THEIR PERFORMANCE AND DRIVE RESULTS THROUGH AUTONOMY AND ACCOUNTABILITY."

EXAMPLE BREAKDOWN

HR RECRUITERS

"DELIVERING EXCEPTIONAL RECRUITING SOLUTIONS THAT ATTRACT TOP TALENT AND SUPPORT BUSINESS GROWTH."

"UTILIZING A DATA-DRIVEN APPROACH TO INFORM RECRUITING STRATEGIES AND ENSURE SUCCESS IN MEETING HIRING GOALS."

"FOSTERING A DIVERSE AND INCLUSIVE CANDIDATE POOL TO PROMOTE EQUITY AND ACCESS FOR ALL CANDIDATES."

"STAYING CURRENT WITH INDUSTRY TRENDS, BEST PRACTICES, AND EMERGING TECHNOLOGIES TO ENSURE THE RECRUITMENT PROCESS IS OPTIMIZED."

"ENSURING COMPLIANCE WITH APPLICABLE LAWS AND REGULATIONS GOVERNING RECRUITMENT AND HIRING PRACTICES."

"FOSTERING A CULTURE OF CONTINUOUS LEARNING AND PROFESSIONAL DEVELOPMENT FOR CANDIDATES AND TEAM MEMBERS."

"DEMONSTRATING A WILLINGNESS TO TAKE CALCULATED RISKS AND MAKE BOLD DECISIONS TO ACHIEVE RECRUITMENT SUCCESSES."

"BUILDING STRONG RELATIONSHIPS WITH INTERNAL STAKEHOLDERS TO SUPPORT RECRUITMENT NEEDS AND OBJECTIVES."

"PROVIDING LEADERSHIP AND GUIDANCE TO OTHER TEAM MEMBERS TO ENSURE THE SUCCESSFUL DELIVERY OF RECRUITMENT GOALS."

EXAMPLE BREAKDOWN

ENTREPRENEUR

"DRIVING INNOVATION AND CHANGE BY CREATING NEW PRODUCTS AND SERVICES THAT SOLVE REAL-WORLD PROBLEMS."

"CREATING A CULTURE OF CREATIVITY, RISK-TAKING, AND EXPERIMENTATION TO FOSTER GROWTH AND SUCCESS."

"DEMONSTRATING A PASSION FOR ENTREPRENEURSHIP AND A DEEP COMMITMENT TO BUILDING A SUCCESSFUL BUSINESS."

"BUILDING STRONG NETWORKS AND PARTNERSHIPS WITH INVESTORS, ADVISORS, AND INDUSTRY LEADERS TO SUPPORT BUSINESS GROWTH."

"INSPIRING AND MOTIVATING TEAM MEMBERS TO ACHIEVE THEIR FULL POTENTIAL AND CONTRIBUTE TO THE SUCCESS OF THE COMPANY."

"EMBRACING DIVERSITY AND INCLUSION AS CORE VALUES AND PROMOTING A CULTURE OF RESPECT AND EQUITY."

"DEMONSTRATING A WILLINGNESS TO TAKE CALCULATED RISKS AND MAKE BOLD DECISIONS TO ACHIEVE SUCCESS."

"LEVERAGING TECHNOLOGY AND DIGITAL MARKETING TO BUILD BRAND AWARENESS AND REACH NEW AUDIENCES."

EXAMPLE BREAKDOWN

JOURNALIST

"PROVIDING ACCURATE, TIMELY, AND ENGAGING NEWS AND STORIES THAT INFORM AND EDUCATE THE PUBLIC."

"DEMONSTRATING A STRONG COMMITMENT TO THE HIGHEST STANDARDS OF JOURNALISM ETHICS AND INTEGRITY."

"UTILIZING DEEP KNOWLEDGE OF INDUSTRIES, MARKETS, AND GLOBAL AFFAIRS TO PRODUCE INFORMATIVE AND INSIGHTFUL NEWS STORIES."

"PROVIDING EXCEPTIONAL WRITING, EDITING, AND STORYTELLING SKILLS TO ENGAGE AND CAPTIVATE AUDIENCES."

"ADVOCATING FOR PRESS FREEDOM, TRANSPARENCY, AND ACCOUNTABILITY IN ALL ASPECTS OF JOURNALISM."

"CREATING THOUGHT-PROVOKING AND IMPACTFUL CONTENT THAT SPARKS CONVERSATION AND DEBATE."

"PROVIDING ADVOCACY AND SUPPORT FOR MARGINALIZED COMMUNITIES AND UNDERREPRESENTED VOICES."

EXAMPLE
BREAKDOWN

NUTRITIONIST

"PROVIDING PERSONALIZED AND INDIVIDUALIZED NUTRITION PLANS THAT ADDRESS THE UNIQUE NEEDS AND PREFERENCES OF EACH CLIENT."

"EMPHASIZING THE IMPORTANCE OF DISEASE PREVENTION, HEALTH PROMOTION, AND HEALTH EDUCATION IN NUTRITION PRACTICE."

"ADVOCATING FOR HEALTH AND WELLNESS THROUGH HEALTHY EATING HABITS AND LIFESTYLE CHOICES."

"PROVIDING GUIDANCE AND SUPPORT TO CLIENTS TO HELP THEM DEVELOP HEALTHY EATING HABITS AND BEHAVIORS THAT SUPPORT THEIR WELLNESS GOALS."

"PROVIDING LEADERSHIP AND MENTORSHIP TO OTHER NUTRITIONISTS AND WELLNESS PROFESSIONALS."

"PROVIDING ADVOCACY AND SUPPORT FOR CLIENTS WITH CHRONIC ILLNESSES AND DISABILITIES RELATED TO NUTRITION AND DIET."

EXAMPLE BREAKDOWN

PERSONAL TRAINER

"HELPING CLIENTS ACHIEVE THEIR FITNESS GOALS THROUGH PERSONALIZED EXERCISE AND NUTRITION PLANS."

"PROVIDING EXPERT KNOWLEDGE OF FITNESS PRACTICES, EXERCISE PHYSIOLOGY, AND NUTRITION TO ENSURE SAFE AND EFFECTIVE TRAINING."

"STAYING UP-TO-DATE WITH THE LATEST RESEARCH, TECHNOLOGIES, AND BEST PRACTICES IN FITNESS TO ENSURE EVIDENCE-BASED TRAINING."

"ADVOCATING FOR HEALTH AND WELLNESS THROUGH PHYSICAL ACTIVITY AND HEALTHY LIFESTYLE HABITS."

"EMPHASIZING THE IMPORTANCE OF INJURY PREVENTION AND PROPER TECHNIQUE TO ENSURE SAFE AND EFFECTIVE TRAINING."

"PROVIDING GUIDANCE AND SUPPORT TO CLIENTS TO HELP THEM DEVELOP HEALTHY HABITS AND BEHAVIORS THAT SUPPORT THEIR FITNESS GOALS."

"CREATING A POSITIVE AND SUPPORTIVE TRAINING ENVIRONMENT THAT FOSTERS A SENSE OF COMMUNITY AND BELONGING."

"PROVIDING LEADERSHIP AND GUIDANCE TO OTHER TRAINERS AND FITNESS PROFESSIONALS TO ENSURE SUCCESS IN ACHIEVING CLIENT GOALS."

"EMPHASIZING THE IMPORTANCE OF SELF-CARE AND RECOVERY IN ACHIEVING FITNESS GOALS, INCLUDING REST, HYDRATION, AND STRETCHING."

Conclusion

Once your value-added statement is written, the hard part is done; you should now have a solid compass that will help to guide you with purpose and make networking and messaging your brand easier.

Your statement can be slotted anywhere you need to market yourself, at the top of your CV, in a cover email or message, on your LinkedIn page, social media bio section, company website, portfolio, or as part of your speaker's bio for introductions.

You can also use it to start an interview or meet and network with people face-to-face. Of course, in person, you don't want to sound like you're just parroting a script, but it's helpful to have a snappy summary to draw on, especially if you're faced with one of those moments where your mind goes blank, and you can't quite think where to begin.

Feel free to tweak and change your value-added statement over time. After all, you are constantly changing and growing, and so should your message.

Chapter Four

Networking

I remember attending my first professional conference. I clutched the itinerary tightly to my chest, raced from room to room to find an empty seat far from everybody else, and then stared at notes or my cell phone until the seminar began.

When the last session ended, I headed straight back to my hotel room, desperate not to make eye contact with anyone on the way.

Thankfully, it didn't take me too long into my career to realize that time spent outside the scheduled seminar was as valuable, if not more than time spent at the workshop.

Painful though it was at first, talking with peers more experienced in my field, who had gathered from all over the country in an informal setting, was crucial to my professional growth and development.

As a twenty-something-year-old trying to grow a business, my objective wasn't to fill a Rolodex (we didn't have social media back then); it was to learn from other's experiences and share my experiences if others had struggles I had overcome.

Thanks to overcoming my shyness and talking to others in network settings, I could call someone in Minnesota or Arizona all the way from South Carolina when I needed expert advice. Years later, I was able to pay it forward and mentor young professionals as they began their own career journeys.

Now that we're on the subject of networking, let's delve further into the importance of networking events. They could be virtual (over Zoom) or in person, networking events, including professional associations, company-sponsored events, or general professional networking groups in your local area.

You might be nervous if you're like me when I first attended a networking event. That's only natural, but there are ways to reduce this anxiety.

For example, you could practice with people you know, such as at PTA meetings or sports events that your kids attend, or with people from work; practice shaking hands and making conversation.

You will want to be approachable, friendly, genuine, and sincere, with a warm smile and a positive, open stance.

When attending a professional networking event, you should be comfortable but professional. Make sure your clothes are clean. Resist the impulse to fidget with your clothes.

You've popped in a breath mint before entering, but you're not chewing gum. Your phone should be on silent. Ensure you've eaten so you're not cranky, and don't treat the refreshment table as a buffet.

If you come with your friends or colleagues, just tell them you'll see them again when you leave. You should avoid sticking close to them the whole time because you intend to meet new people there.

When you come in, have a confident stance, walk in with purpose, look around the room, and take in the atmosphere (I don't want to say these professional networking events are stuffy, but they can be ultra-professional).

Pay attention to your surroundings. Are people shaking hands? Are they fist-bumping? Are they not initiating any contact? Read this behavior. Are people congregating in groups, or are they circulating by themselves? You can walk towards the refreshment table and take all of it in.

If you have somebody in mind that you want to talk to at this event, such as a hiring manager of a company you really want to work for, I suggest you make sure that you don't go directly to them. You want to warm up with other people. Therefore, you also want to look at the attendance list before you go.

If you signed up online, you can research who's coming and those you would like to meet. Who do they work for? Find out a little bit about them so you have something to discuss.

I was interested in connecting with a noted professor early in my career. Excited, I saw she was listed as an attendee at a networking event and looked forward to meeting her and building a rapport.

Before the event, I read several articles she had written. When I approached her at the conference and was able to comment on her publications, I asked questions, which created the opportunity to begin a friendship and be an excellent mentor for years.

When you approach a group, ensure they're not busy in conversation. You don't want to be disruptive, so wait to start talking. Get a feel of the group and the conversation when you come in.

Have your shoulder slightly turned out so that you have a welcoming approach and are part of a circle. And then join in the conversation where there's a natural flow, and you have something to contribute. Ask open-ended questions and participate naturally.

If you're approaching somebody one-on-one, present yourself with a friendly, open demeanor.

If they extend their hand for a handshake, you want to give them a friendly firm handshake; you do not want to turn your hand over. Instead, offer a firm handshake, eye contact, and smile, then follow up with an excellent open-ended question. Or if they start with a question to you, such as "What do you do?" You want to reply with a perfect sixty-second answer with a little bit of a hook.

I think if somebody asked me that question, I would say, "I wanted to be a ballerina, but I ended up as a Director of a Pharmacy, which is probably for the best since I'm better with P&Ls than pirouettes. But I've been in long-term care in the Carolinas for about 20 years leading amazing teams."

Then I return the question to them, "What is it that you do?"

The critical thing to note about my answer is that I briefly stated what I do, what I like, and what my skill set is. Then I would look to add value to their life.

For example, if they say they are heading to Memphis next week. Then suggest some of your favorite barbecue restaurants if you've been there.

Offer to email addresses to a couple of your favorite restaurants. That way, you're giving value and continuing the conversation after the event concludes.

We have five seconds to make an impression. We want to make it a good one, but that sometimes puts a lot of pressure on us and makes us nervous. So, try not to be worried.

Here are some common mistakes that happen when we are nervous.

We tend to overshare.
When we get nervous, it's common to start talking much about ourselves and saying far too much. We do this because we're trying to identify with another person; however, our constant chatter comes across as over-eagerness to reveal too much information about ourselves.

As a result, you end up hogging the conversation. When you find yourself doing this, stop, and ask the person you're conversing with an open-ended question.

We start rambling about something that's not relevant.
Sometimes we can't stop ourselves: we just keep going and going on about something. So at that point, just stop and redirect their

conversation back to them. Ask a question about their company, what they do, or what their favorite part of their job is.

It's a good idea to have a set of questions just in case we freeze up. When you are nervous and feel put on the spot, it is easy to freeze, but if you have a couple of questions in your mind that are your go-to, we can quickly pull that out as our question to break free of the freeze.

I have mentioned that you do not ask for favors, business, or a job at a networking event from someone you have just met. It is acceptable to ask about someone's job but refrain from asking any controversial questions, referring to trade secrets, being gossipy, or encouraging the person to speak ill of competitors.

Make sure you are friendly, genuine, and interested. Everyone knows the unpleasant feeling of talking to someone and realizing they are not listening, so be present in the conversation, not trying to formulate what you want to say next or letting your mind wander.

You want that conversation to last about five minutes. You don't want to monopolize the person, so to disengage from the conversation, you can say something like, "It was great talking with you. I enjoyed learning about your company. I would love to get your card," or "I would love to follow up with you," or "I would love to connect."

Once you get their card, when you are back home, please write about your conversation with them on the back of the card; do not do it in the room in front of them. They'll see you and wonder what the heck it is you're writing about.

Once you get home, write key points and interesting facts about your conversation.

Follow up with a personal note saying that you enjoyed meeting them, the conversation, learning more about their company, or whatever it was you conversed with them about. You'll also follow up by connecting with them on LinkedIn or Twitter.

You always want to be a giver, not a taker.
You want to make sure you are not asking for something when you go to these events. It should be your priority to give value to people and be interested in them, not to make them interested in you.

To give value, listen to what the other person is saying and see how you can help. There may be someone you know whom you could connect with, recommend a restaurant or hotel, or how you have solved a problem similar to what they are facing.

Find networking opportunities through professional associations, local networking opportunities, and companies you're interested in hosting hiring events. Take the time to attend networking events even if you do not feel you will directly benefit.

Each person you connect with broadens your sphere and deepens your roots with your professional colleagues or local community. The person you meet at the Rotary Club may have a former college roommate that is the CEO of your dream company.

Mastering networking skills will always serve you well throughout your life.

Chapter Five

———————∧———————

Messaging Your Brand

What does "messaging your brand" mean?

Everyone you meet will develop an opinion of you and make a superficial judgment of what kind of professional you are. Let it be you who positively shape that vision.

Have you ever been around somebody who's not their authentic self? It's icky and repels you, right?

People don't like phony stuff. Instead, they like authentic people. This creates an interest or tells a story. Therefore, be genuine. You want to share, generate excitement, and form a connection. Ultimately, you will differentiate yourself from others and become known as the subject matter expert.

Think when J Lo went from a fly girl to an actress, to a singer, or Mark Wahlberg went from a singer, to an actor, to an entrepreneur. Branding is for more than just actors. It is for anybody who wants to transition and show that they are an expert and a valid professional for that role.

To be memorable, we must be unique and warm and consistently demonstrate our expertise.

You have determined our brand and what you want to be known for and distilled it concisely into your personal brand statement. Now we will discuss how to communicate, manage, and message it correctly.

Find your goal.

Start by defining your overall objectives for using social media. Common goals include increasing brand awareness, driving website traffic, generating leads or sales, fostering customer engagement, or establishing thought leadership.

Ensure your goals are Specific, Measurable, Achievable, Relevant, and Time-bound (SMART). For example, instead of setting a vague goal like "increase followers," set a SMART goal like "increase Instagram followers by 20% over the next six months."

Key Performance Indicators (KPIs) will play a crucial role in tracking and evaluating the success of your branding efforts. KPIs related to brand awareness assess how well your target audience recognizes and recalls your brand. Examples of brand awareness KPIs include:

Reach and Impressions: Measure the number of people exposed to your brand or content, such as the reach of your social media posts or the number of impressions your advertisements receive.

Brand Mentions: Track the number of times your brand is mentioned online, including social media mentions, media coverage, or customer reviews.

Social Media Followers: Monitor the growth of your social media audience to gauge your brand's visibility and appeal.

Website Traffic: Analyze the number of visitors to your website and track how many are new users, indicating the effectiveness of your brand exposure.

Social Media Engagement: Track the likes, comments, shares, and overall engagement on your social media posts. This reflects the level of interaction and interest your content generates.

Find your audience.

Whether you're in marketing or engineering, we will keep our messaging related to our brand and our audience.

For example, as a Geriatric Nurse Practitioner, your audience could be healthcare colleagues, pharmaceutical companies, professional associations, patients, or regulators in the senior health space.

Find your voice.

Now, find your voice. Share information and your journey, and be relatable, authentic, and genuine.

Do not try to be like someone else that is popular. You will have credibility and create excitement and connections based on who you are, not whom you are trying to be like.

Types of Social Media Content

Social media content comes in a variety of formats to engage your audience. The main types of content are educational, entertaining, informational, inspirational, interactive, user-generated, behind-the-scenes, and promotional.

Promotional Content: This content directly markets a product, service, or event. The goal of promotional content is to persuade your audience to make a purchase or take a specific action.

Examples:

- **Referral Program:** "Refer a Friend & Earn Discounts for Referrals"

- **Free Trial Offer:** "Try Our Premium Membership Free For 7 Days!"

- **Loyalty Program:** "VIP Membership: Unlock Exclusive Benefits and Rewards"

Informational Content: This content shares essential information or news about your industry, brand, or products. It keeps your audience informed and aware.

Example:

- **Expert Interview on a Podcast:** "Leadership Insights: Interview with a Fortune 500 CEO"

- **Fact-Filled Infographic:** "The Most Interesting Facts About Iguanas"

- **Educational YouTube Video:** "Phlebotomists: The Undiscovered Career"

Educational Content: Educational content aims to teach your audience something new or provide them with knowledge about a particular topic. This type of content can help you position your brand as an industry authority.

Example:

- **Infographic:** "A Ranking of The 10 Best Pies In America"

- **Blog Post:** "How AI Is Affecting Higher Education. Cheating or Adapting?"

- **Podcast:** "The Science Behind Methane and Climate Change"

Entertaining Content: Entertaining content is to amuse your audience, often with humor or creativity. This type of content is effective for humanizing your brand and engaging with your audience on a more personal level.

Example:

- **Instagram Story:** "Guess the Movie Based On My Interpretive Dance"

- **Twitter Thread:** "Most Embarrassing High School Moment"

- **Caption Contest:** "Caption This! Funny Animal Edition"

Inspirational Content: This type of content seeks to motivate, inspire, or provoke emotion in your audience. It's a powerful way to create a positive association with your brand.

Example:

- **Motivational Webinar:** "Unlock Your Potential, Strategies for Personal Growth"

- **Facebook:** "30-Day Gratitude Challenge: Post A Pic Every Day of Something/Someone You Are Grateful For"

- **Blog:** "From Homeless to Hopeful: A Story of Transformation"

User-Generated Content (UGC): UGC is content created by your audience. It's a powerful way to engage your community and showcase your customers' experiences.

Example:

- **Instagram Contest:** "Share Your Trip for A Chance To Win a Trip!"

- **Stories:** "Our Client Success Stories: Video Testimonials"

- **LinkedIn:** "What Our Customers Love About Us"

Behind-The-Scenes Content: This content offers a glimpse into the inner workings of your brand, giving your audience a feel for your brand's personality and values.

Example:

- **Instagram Stories:** "Inside the World of Beauty: Behind the Runway Show"

- **Pinterest:** "Closet Makeover: Stunning Before-and-After Photos"

- **Facebook Live:** "Q&A While I Put On Our New Makeup Line"

Interactive Content: Interactive content encourages your audience to actively engage, often through quizzes, polls, contests, or question boxes.

Example:

- **LinkedIn Poll:** "Cover Letter or No Cover Letter?"

- **Livestream:** "Trivia: Who Knows the Most About Random Insect Facts?"

- **Interactive Storytelling:** "The Interactive Mystery: Help Solve the Case"

EDUCATIONAL CONTENT	• INFOGRAPHICS THAT VISUALLY EXPLAIN COMPLEX TOPICS. • STEP-BY-STEP TUTORIALS AND HOW-TO GUIDES. • LISTICLES THAT PROVIDE HELPFUL TIPS AND ADVICE. • INDUSTRY NEWS AND UPDATES. • EXPLAINER VIDEOS THAT BREAK DOWN COMPLEX CONCEPTS.
INSPIRATIONAL CONTENT	• MOTIVATIONAL QUOTES AND MESSAGES • INSPIRING SUCCESS STORIES AND CASE STUDIES. • INSPIRATIONAL VIDEOS AND CLIPS. • EXAMPLES OF PEOPLE OVERCOMING CHALLENGES AND ADVERSITY. • IMAGES AND VIDEOS THAT SHOWCASE BEAUTIFUL OR AWE-INSPIRING SCENERY.
PERSONAL CONTENT	• BEHIND-THE-SCENES GLIMPSES OF YOUR DAILY LIFE AND ROUTINE. • PERSONAL STORIES AND EXPERIENCES THAT SHOWCASE YOUR PERSONALITY AND VALUES. • PHOTOS AND VIDEOS OF YOUR PETS, FAMILY, AND HOBBIES. • HUMOROUS POSTS AND MEMES THAT SHOWCASE YOUR SENSE OF HUMOR. • PERSONAL REFLECTIONS AND MUSINGS ON LIFE AND CURRENT EVENTS.
BEHIND-THE-SCENES CONTENT	• SNEAK PEEKS OF UPCOMING PROJECTS AND PRODUCTS. • BEHIND-THE-SCENES PHOTOS AND VIDEOS OF YOUR CREATIVE PROCESS. • Q&A SESSIONS WITH MEMBERS OF YOUR TEAM OR INDUSTRY EXPERTS. • LIVE STREAMS OF EVENTS OR BEHIND-THE-SCENES MOMENTS. • TIME LAPSE VIDEOS THAT SHOWCASE THE WORK THAT GOES INTO CREATING YOUR CONTENT.
USER-GENERATED CONTENT	• TESTIMONIALS OR REVIEWS. • PHOTOS OR VIDEOS THAT FEATURE YOUR AUDIENCE USING YOUR PRODUCT OR SERVICE.

Find your content.

The content category's objectives include:

Attraction: to help you reach new audiences.

Authority: to build trust as an expert.

Affinity: to be a brand people want to be around and share beliefs

Action: to create an interested audience of customers.

In the example of the Geriatric Nurse Practitioner, your content's focus is senior health issues. These include topics related to long-term care, regulatory matters, or updated pharmacy issues that concern the geriatric population.

Help the audience understand what you do beyond a title so that they benefit from the value you bring.

Ideas include:

Common health conditions that affect the elderly, such as osteoporosis, arthritis, and dementia.

Strategies for preventing falls in older adults.

How to recognize and manage depression in older adults.

The role of hospice and palliative care in end-of-life care for older adults.

The benefits of pet therapy for older adults.

Find your form.

Content is delivered in multiple forms, including blogs, videos, infographics, podcasts, white papers, and books (eBooks, audio, paperback, or hardcover). You can create these or reshare others' articles or posts, providing a link to their original work.

Find your outlet.

You are your brand, so networking events and speaking engagements are excellent ways to relay your professional brand.

Collaborating with other experts through their podcasts, videos, and academic events, will message your brand, help gain access to a greater audience, and collaboration further increases social proof.

Social media channels are the most convenient and consistent way to message your personal brand. With many platforms out there, let's take a deeper look at the types of social media and content appropriate for each forum so that you can make the best match of your brand and voice to the channels available.

Choose the Right Platforms.

Various social media platforms are available, including Twitter, Instagram, LinkedIn, Pinterest, Tik Tok, Snapchat, YouTube, Reddit, Tumblr, Clubhouse, Twitch, WeChat, WhatsApp, and more, to message your brand. The best platform will be the one that aligns with YOUR personal brand and target audience.

Different platforms have different audiences and content formats. For example, Tik Tok is a highly visual platform popular among younger audiences, while LinkedIn is a text-based platform popular among professionals.

Start with one or two platforms and focus on creating high-quality content for those platforms.

Cross-promote.

Once you have gained an audience on your chosen social platform, it is essential to continue to grow and maximize your reach.

One way to foster growth on a new channel is to encourage your existing audience to follow you on other social media.

Let's say you're a small business owner, and you have a Facebook page with a following of 5,000 people. But your Instagram following is much smaller, with only 50 followers.

Here are some steps you can take:

1. Create a post that promotes your Instagram account, encourages your followers to follow you on Instagram, and includes a link to your profile.

2. To incentivize your Facebook followers to follow you on Instagram, offer exclusive content on your Instagram account that is not available on your Facebook page. For example, you could share behind-the-scenes photos, sneak peeks of new products, or exclusive promotions on your Instagram account.

3. Run a contest that requires participants to follow you on Instagram. You can promote this contest on your Facebook page and require participants to follow you on Instagram to be eligible to win. The prize can be related to your business, such as a gift card or a free product.

4. Use hashtags on both Facebook and Instagram relevant to your business and industry to help your target audience find you on both platforms.

5. Finally, it's crucial to maintain consistent branding across both platforms to help your audience recognize and connect with your brand. Use the same logo, colors, and tone of voice on Facebook and Instagram to create a consistent brand identity.

Create High-Quality Content.

The key to establishing your personal brand is high-quality content that is engaging and valuable to your audience. This will help you stand out and build a loyal following.

Consider the following tips when creating content.

Visuals are an essential part of social media content. Use images or videos that align with your personal brand and are visually appealing. You can use tools like Canva or Adobe Spark to create visually stunning graphics.

Write engaging captions that grab your audience's attention and communicate your message effectively. Use storytelling techniques, ask questions, or use humor to make your captions more engaging.

Hashtags are an excellent way to increase your reach and connect with your target audience. Use relevant hashtags that align with your content and are popular among your target audience.

Instagram allows up to 30 hashtags per post, but the optimal number of hashtags is between 9 and 11. Using too many hashtags can come across as spammy while using too few can limit the visibility of your post.

Twitter allows up to 280 characters per tweet, so it's essential to keep your hashtags brief. One to two hashtags per tweet are generally sufficient.

Threads allow 500 characters and ten media items, including links, photos, and videos, but do not utilize hashtags.

Facebook's algorithm places less importance on hashtags than other platforms, so it's generally best to use just one or two relevant hashtags per post.

LinkedIn allows up to 3 hashtags per post, and it's best to use hashtags relevant to your industry or the topic of your post.

Keep in mind that content is essential, but quality should not be sacrificed for the sake of quantity.

If that means you only post one high-quality post per week instead of substantive material daily, always choose quality — you will earn the respect of your audience and enhance your brand.

Engage With Your Audience.
Engagement is a term used to describe the level of interaction and activity between social media users and the content they see on social media platforms.

Engagement measures the number of likes, comments, shares, and other forms of interaction that users have with social media content.

Engagement is vital to building a loyal following and establishing your personal brand as an influencer.

It's important to not only create content but also to respond to comments and messages and encourage your audience to engage with your content. It is also essential to participate in conversations and collaborate with others in your industry or field.

The first 15 minutes after you post content is the most powerful driver for the platforms' algorithm. If there is good engagement, likes, shares, and comments, the algorithm will determine your valuable content and push it in front of a greater audience. Therefore, it is essential to post at peak times your audience is viewing and engaging with them.

You also need to engage with your audience to build relationships with them, understand their needs, and help establish yourself as a thought leader in your niche.

Timing

When structuring your branding messaging plan, timing is a key aspect. What social interaction, including content creation, can you reasonably and consistently execute? Can you commit to posting a thread three times a day, or is once a day more realistic?

But it is essential to produce high-quality content, even if it's less quantity, instead of a large volume of average quality. Your creative, unique content captures attention, sparks interest, and encourages users to follow you.

Write the cadence in a content calendar and stick with the plan. Believe me; your audience will begin looking for your posts. Consistency builds trust and loyalty.

Your plan should include determining the time of day you post your thread. There will be speculation about what time of day is the best for the platform, but the best time of day is the best time for your audience.

For my personal Instagram audience, the metrics suggested 9 am until 11 am on Wednesday mornings was the ideal time, but the most convenient for me was 5 am before I rolled out of bed. Before I brushed my teeth, I would have over 100 likes.

Time to Post

The bottom line, the best time to post a thread is a time you know you can be consistent with and connects best with your audience.

Also, evaluate the time of day your audience engages with your content. According to hootsuite.com, the best time to post on social media overall is noon EST on Mondays. But every platform and audience has its own peak.

By social platform in Eastern Standard Time (EST) according to socialsprout.com:

Best times to post on Facebook: Mondays through Fridays at 2 a.m., Tuesdays at 9 a.m., and noon

Best days to post on Facebook: Tuesdays through Fridays

Worst days to post on Facebook: Saturdays

Best times to post on Instagram: Mondays at noon, Tuesdays and Wednesdays from 11 a.m. to 2 p.m., and Thursdays and Fridays 11 a.m. and 12:00 p.m.

Best days to post on Instagram: Tuesdays and Wednesdays

Worst days to post on Instagram: Sundays

Best times to post on TikTok: Tuesdays, 3–4 p.m., and Wednesdays and Thursdays, 2–3 p.m.

Best days to post on TikTok: Wednesdays and Thursdays

Worst days to post on TikTok: Sundays

Best times to post on Twitter: Monday, Tuesday, Wednesday, Fridays, and Saturdays at 10 a.m.

Best days to post on Twitter: Tuesdays and Wednesdays

Worst days to post on Twitter: Sundays

Best times to post on LinkedIn: Tuesdays, 11 a.m.–1 p.m.

Best days to post on LinkedIn: Wednesdays and Thursdays

Worst days to post on LinkedIn: Saturdays and Sundays

The first 15 minutes after you post content is the most powerful driver for the platforms' algorithm. If there is good engagement, likes, shares, and comments, the algorithm will determine your valuable content and push it in front of a greater audience. Therefore, it is important to post at peak times your audience is viewing and engaging with them.

If you receive a comment, immediately comment back. This also stimulates the algorithm and encourages others to participate also.

Content Calendar

To stay consistent, a vital tool will be your content calendar. It allows you to have an overhead view of days, weeks, or months' worth of content to ensure you are creating valuable, diverse, and thoughtful threads. The spreadsheet should include the following elements:

- An outline of what each post is about.

- When you plan to publish the content.

- Which platform the content is intended for.

- The content type if it's a blog post, video, image, infographic, etc.

- Any images, videos, or other media associated with the post.

- The exact text that will accompany your content.

- Then keep track of the performance of each post (likes, shares, comments, etc.) after it's been published.

Automating Social Media Posting with Applications

Some great apps automate social media posting, provide analytics and other valuable features. A few:

- <u>Hootsuite</u>: A widely used platform that allows scheduling posts for all major social media networks and provides analytics to measure content performance.

- <u>Buffer</u>: This tool is known for its easy-to-use interface and Instagram direct posting feature. A nice feature is a built-in image creator.

- <u>Sprout Social</u>: Offers social media management tools, analytics, and a calendar that allows for scheduling, queueing, and drafting of posts.

- <u>Later</u>: This tool is best for visual platforms like Instagram and Pinterest, offering a visual content calendar, scheduling features, and a link-in-bio tool for Instagram.

Track Your Metrics.

Regularly monitoring your metrics helps you understand your target audience and improve their desired content.

Many tools are available to monitor social media metrics depending on your needs and preferences.

Some of the metrics you will want to analyze include:

Engagement Rate: Track your engagement rate to understand how your audience interacts with your content.

Follower Growth: Track your follower growth to understand how your audience grows over time.

Website Traffic: Use Google Analytics to track website traffic from your social media channels.

Lead Generation: Track how many leads you generate from your social media channels.

Also, consider competitor analysis and audience demographics.

Conclusion

Your social media content should be engaging, interesting, interactive, inspiring, educational, fun, or engaging and in line with your brand. Consider your audience, the platform the appropriate media for the platform.

Use your authentic voice and a mix of content that will attract an audience, nurture, and grow through bringing them value, then mix in promoting your product or service. Building your brand is about building a community and forming relationships. The growth of a following and sales of products and services will develop from the seeds of connections.

Instagram

Instagram is one of the most popular social media platforms, with over 1 billion monthly active users and over 500 million daily users.

According to a 2021 survey by the Pew Research Center, the average age of Instagram users is between 18 and 34 years old. Instagram is a highly visual platform, so it's essential to create high-quality visual content that resonates with your target audience.

Use clear and bright images that showcase your content and add text overlays to make them more shareable. Post consistently, engage with your audience, and optimize your bio.

Some vital statistics about Instagram

71% of Instagram's users are under the age of 35.

_____

_____

79% of users on Instagram are more likely to purchase after seeing a product or service on the platform.

_____

_____

Influencer marketing on Instagram is a billion-dollar industry, with brands spending an estimated $8 billion on influencer marketing in 2020.

_____

_____

Instagram users engage with brand content at a rate of 4x higher than on Facebook.

_____

_____

Posts with hashtags receive an average of 12.6% more engagement than posts without hashtags.

_____

_____

The best kinds of content to post on Instagram are visually appealing and provide value to your audience:

    ⬡   Lifestyle and personal photos

- ☐ Behind-the-scenes glimpses of your work process or creative process

- ☐ Inspirational quotes and affirmations

- ☐ Product reviews and recommendations

- ☐ Tutorials and how-to guides

Facebook

Facebook is an extremely popular social media platform with over 2.7 billion monthly active users that allows users to connect with friends and family, join groups, and follow pages. Users spend an average of 20 hours per month, according to datareportal.com.

Best kinds of content.

The best kinds of content to post on Facebook are visually appealing and provide value to your audience. Approximately 43% of U.S. adults get their news from Facebook, according to a 2021 survey by Pew Research Center.

Some ideas:

- Personal thoughts and opinions on industry news or trends.

- Behind-the-scenes glimpses of your work process or creative process.

- Inspirational quotes and affirmations.

- Product reviews and recommendations.

- Tutorials and how-to guides.

Optimize your profile.

Optimizing your profile is the first step to messaging your brand on Facebook. Use a professional profile picture that reflects your personal brand.

Write a bio that accurately represents who you are and what you offer, with keywords to help your profile appear in search results.

Use a consistent brand aesthetic across all platforms, such as a color scheme or header image, to help your audience recognize your brand.

Best times and days to post.

The best times and days to post on Facebook can vary depending on your niche and target audience. However, here are some general guidelines:

- Best times to post on Facebook: Mondays through Fridays at 2 a.m., Tuesdays at 9 a.m., and noon.

- The best days to post on Facebook are Tuesday through Friday.

- The worst day to post on Facebook is Saturday.

- Post consistently, such as once a day or three times a week, to help build a loyal following and increase engagement.

Facebook can be a powerful tool for messaging your brand and reaching a wider audience. By optimizing your profile, creating high-quality visual content, engaging with your audience, and posting at the correct times, you can build a strong presence on Facebook and increase your reach and engagement.

Podcast

With over 2 million active podcasts and over 100 million Americans listening to podcasts, this social platform has become a popular medium to message your personal brand. There is a growing audience for podcast content and an opportunity to share your knowledge, experiences, and perspectives with your target audience.

Tips on Podcasting:

_____

_____

Speak with a conversational tone to engage with your audience to create a connection.

_____

_____

Use a consistent intro and outro that reflects your brand and helps your audience recognizes your podcast.

_____

_____

Engagement is vital to messaging your brand on a podcast; encourage your audience to submit questions and feedback through social media or email.

_____

_____

Use listener feedback to guide your content and improve your podcast.

Participate in podcasting communities and collaborate with other influencers or brands in your niche.

The best kinds of content to share on a podcast align with your personal brand and provide value to your audience. Some ideas:

- ☐ Interviews with other influencers or industry experts

- ☐ Personal stories and experiences

- ☐ Educational content, such as how-to guides or tutorials

- ☐ Product reviews and recommendations

- ☐ Q&A sessions and listener feedback

Pinterest

With over 400 million active users and over 200 billion pins, Pinterest is a highly visual search engine that can help you reach a wider audience and drive more traffic to your website or blog.

Tips on Pinterest:

Use clear and bright images that showcase your content and add text overlays to make them more shareable.

Use Pinterest's guided search feature to find relevant keywords and hashtags for your pins.

Curate and pin content from other experts, brands, or sources that align with your personal brand.

_____

_____

Use illustrative board titles and descriptions to help your content appear in the search results.

_____

_____

Engagement is critical to messaging your brand on Pinterest, responding to comments

and messages, and re-pin content from other users.

_____

_____

Participate in group boards and collaborate with other brands in your niche to increase your reach.

_____

_____

Use Pinterest analytics to track and optimize your engagement, reach, and audience demographics.

_____

_____

The best times and days to post on Pinterest can vary depending on your niche and target audience. However, here are some general guidelines:

- The best time to post on Pinterest is during off-work hours, such as evenings or weekends.

- The best days to post on Pinterest are Saturdays and Sundays.

- Pin consistently throughout the day to reach users in different time zones.

- The best times to post on Pinterest are Saturday morning, Friday afternoon, and evening, and Sundays at 5 p.m.

_____

_____

The best type of content to post on Pinterest includes:

- Blog posts and articles

- Infographics and data visualizations

- Videos and tutorials

- Inspirational quotes and affirmations

- Product reviews and recommendations

- How-to guides and tips

Pinterest is a popular search engine that can be a powerful tool for messaging your brand and reaching a wider audience.

YouTube

YouTube can be a powerful platform for messaging your brand and showcasing your content. With over 2 billion monthly active users and over 1 billion hours of video watched every day, YouTube is the second-largest search engine in the world. It is a powerful tool for building your personal brand.

Tips on YouTube:

Create content that aligns with your personal brand and provides value to your audience. An iPhone and video editing app is equipment enough to get started.

_____

_____

Write a keyword-rich channel description that accurately represents who you are and what you offer.

_____

_____

Use keywords in your video titles, descriptions, and tags to help your content appear in search results.

_____

_____

Engagement is critical to messaging your brand on YouTube; respond to comments and messages and encourage your audience to engage with your content.

_____

_____

Participate in the YouTube community by subscribing to other channels and collaborating with other influencers or brands in your niche.

The best times and days to post on YouTube can vary depending on your niche and target audience. However, here are some general guidelines:

- ☐ The best days to post on YouTube are Thursdays and Fridays, and the best time to post is between 2–4 p.m.

- ☐ Post consistently (once a week or twice a month) to help build a loyal following and increase engagement.

The best types of content align with your personal brand and provide value to your audience. Here are some ideas:

- ☐ Vlogs and day-in-the-life videos.

- ☐ How-to tutorials and product reviews.

- ☐ Q&A sessions, live streams, or interviews with other influencers or industry experts.

You don't need to be perfect to get started on YouTube. Cross-promote from your other social media channels, engage, and collaborate with others in your field, share valuable content, and post on a consistent but comfortable cadence.

Over time, using a high-quality camera, microphone, professional channel banner, and profile picture that reflects your personal brand to create high-quality video content will increase your audience and professional brand. However, it is optional to get started.

Twitter

Twitter is a popular social media platform that allows users to share short messages, known as tweets, with their followers.

Some vital statistics about Twitter

Twitter has 330 million monthly active users.

According to Pew Research, 42% of Twitter users in the United States are college-educated, and 38% have an annual household income of $75,000 or more.

The percentage of users by age is:

- 18–29 years old: 44%

- 30–49 years old: 27%

- 50–64 years old: 18%

- 65 years old and above 8%

There are around 500 million tweets sent per day on Twitter.

Tweets with images or videos receive 150% more retweets.

The best times to post on Twitter are during off-work hours, such as in the evenings or on weekends, and the best days to post on Twitter are Wednesdays and Thursdays.

Tweet consistently, 3–5 times daily, to help build a loyal following and increase engagement.

Twitter allows a maximum of 280 characters per tweet; this limit includes any URLs, usernames, emojis, or images that are included in the tweet. Therefore, use clear and concise language that conveys your message effectively.

Twitter allows a maximum of 280 characters per tweet; this limit includes any URLs, usernames, emojis, or images that are included in the tweet. Therefore, use clear and concise language that conveys your message effectively.

_____

_____

Tweets that use hashtags receive 100% more engagement than those without, so select relevant hashtags to help your tweets appear in search results.

_____

_____

The best kinds of content include:

- ☐ Personal thoughts and opinions on industry news or trends

- ☐ Quick tips and tricks related to your niche

- ⍰ Questions that prompt engagement and conversation with your audience

- ⍰ Retweets and shoutouts to other experts or brands in your niche

- ⍰ Shareable quotes and motivational messages

Twitter can be a powerful tool for messaging your brand and reaching a wider audience. By optimizing your profile, creating high-quality written content, engaging with your audience, and posting at the correct times, you can build a strong presence on Twitter and increase your reach and engagement.

LinkedIn

Your LinkedIn profile is one of the most powerful tools in your digital arsenal. As a social media platform, it is primarily geared toward professional networking, and that's precisely how you want to use it.

You are going to want to give your profile a refresh from top to bottom.

Your Profile

A survey of recruiters and hiring managers revealed that potential employees look at your LinkedIn profile when they're considering hiring you; more than 90% of recruiters search for candidates on LinkedIn.

Upload a professional profile picture that presents you as approachable and friendly, e.g., smiling and relaxed.

_____

_____

The photo will consist of your head and shoulders with a plain background (it will not feature your spouse, dog, or rowdy friends). The size of the profile of the picture is 400 x 400 pixels .jpg. This will allow for a high-quality image.

You can use one of the premade banners that LinkedIn has available, or you can create and upload custom ones (the latter is recommended).

To create a custom banner, you can create a free account on Canva, a "free-to-use online graphic design tool. And select the appropriate size dimensions for a custom LinkedIn banner (1586 x 396). Then you can choose one of the templates, upload your picture, and edit for a clean, professional look.

Set your profile to public so that anybody can look at it.

Special Features
A new feature you can add to your profile is a video displayed with your profile picture. It will display a 3-second muted preview, then revert to your profile picture. If a LinkedIn member wants to see more, they can click on the profile picture for a video up to 30 seconds long. This feature is another tool to message your brand; on the downside, if not executed well, it could be a negative.

Change your URL from the randomly assigned www.linkedin.com/in/xxxxx to a shorter, more personalized address, such as www.linkedin.com/in/cathyeppspharmd. This will give your resume, business cards, and email signature line a more professional and polished look.

Make sure your profile also has your city and state. You are 23 times more likely to get discovered by recruiters in searches.

Write An Eye-Catching Profile Headline

The profile headline will be the first thing people read. It needs to contain keywords and summarize your personal brand. Employers typically only spend 7 to 10 seconds reviewing a LinkedIn profile.

Therefore, it is essential to make a solid first impression and ensure that the most important information is easily accessible and highlighted in the profile. Create a bold and clear headline that introduces curiosity to encourage people to click on your profile, engage, and connect.

Important components of your headline include keywords, strengths, and personality. Keywords are what recruiters are going to use to search for you. There is a limit of 220 characters for a headline, but only the first 60 will show on the postings of comments.

When a recruiter is looking for a clinical pharmacist, those are the keywords they'll use. If this is a position that you want, use keyword density. That will put you at the top of the list. Therefore, put the words "clinical pharmacist" in that summary several times throughout your page, bumping you closer to the top of a search.

If you're not sure of the keyword that you want to use, look for somebody else's profile in your industry and how they use their profiles. For example, if you wish for a Chief Financial Officer position, perform a keyword search and look at profile headings of those who come up under CFO for inspiration.

Also, look at the companies that you want to work for. Look at what kind of keywords they use in the description of their company, and then mimic those. This is because those are the ones they will be searching with.

The Summary Section

Your summary should be a brief overview of your professional experience and skills. It must include keywords relevant to your industry and highlight your unique selling points.

Instead, this is your chance to show your voice, talent, strong communication style, and ambitions that differ from your current job sphere.

To show what kind of value you provide and what you bring to the table. This is a perfect place to insert your value into its statement.

20 LinkedIn headlines and summary statements for pharmacists to make your profile stand out

1- Clinical Pharmacist

Profile Headline: Clinical Pharmacist | Patient-Centered Care | Medication Optimization | Health Outcomes

Or

Profile Headline: Clinical Pharmacist | Evidence-Based Practice | Collaborative Care | Medication Therapy Management

Summary:

As a clinical pharmacist with over eight years of experience, I am dedicated to improving patient outcomes through evidence-based practices. I have a strong background in medication therapy management, drug information, and clinical research. My expertise includes pharmacokinetics, pharmacodynamics, and drug interactions. I am also experienced in collaborating with healthcare providers to optimize patient medication regimens and improve patient safety. With a proven track record of success in diverse clinical settings, I am confident I can make a meaningful impact on patient health and well-being.

2- Pharmacy Informatics

Profile Headline: Experienced Pharmacist| Informatics Specialist | Leveraging Technology to Optimize Medication Use and Improve Patient Outcomes

Summary:

As a pharmacist with a passion for technology and data analysis, I am seeking opportunities to transition into a pharmacy informatics specialist role. I have a strong foundation in medication management, clinical decision support, and healthcare information technology. I am also experienced in data analysis and visualization and have been actively pursuing continuing education in pharmacy informatics topics. My goal is to leverage my experience and knowledge to optimize medication use and improve patient outcomes through the use of technology and data-driven insights.

3- Medical Writer

Profile Headline: Medical Writer | Scientific Writing | Medical Communications | Regulatory Compliance | Editing | Content Development

Summary:

As a skilled Medical Writer, I am dedicated to translating complex scientific information into clear and concise content for various audiences. My expertise lies in scientific writing, medical communications, regulatory compliance, editing, and content development. I have a proven track record of successfully developing and editing scientific manuscripts, regulatory documents, and medical education materials. I excel in conducting thorough research and analysis to ensure accuracy and adherence to regulatory requirements. I am passionate about staying up-to-date with the latest medical and scientific advancements and utilizing the latest technologies to develop and deliver high-quality content.

4- Clinical Trials Specialist

Profile Headline: Clinical Trials Expert | Driving Innovation and Advancing Patient Care through Research

Summary:

With extensive experience in clinical trials, I am passionate about driving innovation and advancing patient care through research. I deeply understand the drug development process, from preclinical studies to post-marketing surveillance. I am skilled in all aspects of clinical trial design, implementation, and analysis. Whether working with a pharmaceutical company, a contract research organization, or an academic institution, my goal is to ensure that clinical trials are conducted safely, ethically, and efficiently and that the results are meaningful and impactful for patients and healthcare providers.

5- Medical Science Liaison

Profile Headline: Medical Science Liaison | Bridging the Gap Between Science and Clinical Practice to Improve Patient Outcomes

Summary:

As a medical science liaison, I am dedicated to bridging the gap between the latest scientific research and clinical practice. I work closely with healthcare providers, researchers, and other stakeholders to ensure that the most up-to-date and accurate information is available to inform clinical decision-making and improve patient outcomes. With a deep understanding of the latest developments in medical science and the regulatory and commercial landscape, I can provide valuable insights and support to a wide range of stakeholders. Whether I am developing educational materials, presenting at scientific conferences, or collaborating with cross-functional teams, my goal is always to ensure that patients receive the best possible care based on the latest evidence and best practices.

6- Engineer

Profile Headline: Engineer | Design and Development | Project Management | Innovation | Problem Solving | Collaborative Teamwork

Summary:

As an experienced Engineer, I am dedicated to designing and developing innovative solutions to complex engineering problems while utilizing my project management and collaborative teamwork skills. My expertise lies in product design and development, project management, innovation, and problem-solving. I have a proven track record of successfully managing engineering projects from concept to launch, utilizing the latest engineering tools and technologies to deliver optimal results. I excel in collaboration with interdisciplinary teams to develop creative solutions to complex engineering problems. I am passionate about staying up-to-date with the latest engineering trends and best practices to ensure the success of my projects and the organization. I am committed to building solid relationships with clients and colleagues, delivering projects on time and within budget, and adhering to the highest ethical standards.

7- Compliance Officer

Profile Headline: Compliance Officer | Regulatory Compliance | Risk Management | Policy Development | Auditing | Training and Education

Summary:

As an experienced Compliance Officer, I am dedicated to ensuring organizational compliance with regulatory requirements and mitigating risks through effective risk management. My expertise lies in policy development, auditing, and training and education. I have a proven track record of successfully developing and implementing compliance programs, conducting audits to identify areas of non-compliance, and delivering practical compliance training to employees. I excel in conducting thorough risk assessments and developing strategies to mitigate risks while ensuring compliance with regulatory requirements. I am passionate about staying up-to-date with the latest regulatory trends and requirements to ensure compliance and reduce risk. I am committed to building solid relationships with stakeholders, including regulators, auditors, and employees, to ensure organizational compliance and risk mitigation. If you are looking for a Compliance Officer who can ensure regulatory compliance and reduce risk through effective policy development, auditing, training, and education, I am ready to help.

8- Medical Resident

Profile Headline: Medical Resident | Clinical Expertise | Patient Care | Medical Research | Collaborative Teamwork | Professional Development

Summary:

As a Medical Resident, I am dedicated to providing high-quality patient care while developing my clinical expertise and contributing to medical research. I have a passion for learning and am committed to ongoing professional development. I excel in collaborating with interdisciplinary healthcare teams to provide holistic patient care. I am skilled in conducting medical research and presenting findings at conferences and publications. I am dedicated to adhering to the highest ethical standards and utilizing evidence-based medicine to inform patient care. As a Medical Resident, I am committed to providing compassionate and competent patient care while developing my skills and contributing to advancing medical knowledge.

9- Outcomes Pharmacist

Profile Headline: Outcomes Pharmacist | Driving Quality Improvement and Enhancing Patient Care

Summary:

As an Outcomes Pharmacist, I am dedicated to driving quality improvement and enhancing patient care. By leveraging my expertise in pharmacotherapy, medication safety, and healthcare analytics, I can identify opportunities to improve patient outcomes and optimize medication use. Whether it's conducting medication therapy management, analyzing clinical data, or collaborating with other healthcare team members, I am committed to providing the highest level of patient-centered care. Through my work in quality improvement initiatives, I am able to develop and implement strategies to improve medication safety, reduce adverse drug events, and enhance patient satisfaction.

10- Nurse Practitioner

Profile Headline: Nurse Practitioner | Primary Care | Clinical Expertise | Patient Assessment | Treatment Planning | Health Promotion

Summary:

As a skilled Nurse Practitioner, I am dedicated to providing comprehensive primary care services to patients of all ages while utilizing my clinical expertise and patient assessment skills. I am passionate about promoting health and wellness and developing personalized treatment plans that meet each patient's unique needs. I excel in collaboration with interdisciplinary healthcare teams to provide holistic patient care. I am skilled in performing physical examinations, diagnosing and treating acute and chronic illnesses, and prescribing medications. I am dedicated to adhering to the highest ethical standards and utilizing evidence-based nursing practices to inform patient care. I am committed to ongoing professional development and staying up-to-date with the latest nursing trends and best practices. As a Nurse Practitioner, I am committed to providing high-quality, patient-centered care to improve the health and well-being of my patients.

11- Medication Therapy Management Pharmacist

Profile Headline: Medication Therapy Management Pharmacist | Improving Patient Outcomes through Comprehensive Medication Reviews and Personalized Care

Summary:

As a Medication Therapy Management Pharmacist, I am dedicated to improving patient outcomes through comprehensive medication reviews and personalized care. By working closely with patients and their healthcare providers, I am able to identify and resolve medication-related problems, optimize medication therapy, and improve adherence to prescribed regimens. Through my expertise in pharmacotherapy and patient counseling, I can provide patients with the knowledge and skills they need to manage their medications effectively and achieve their health goals.

12- Long Term Care Consultant Pharmacist

Profile Headline: Long-Term Care Consultant Pharmacist | Improving Quality of Life for Seniors through Comprehensive Medication Management

Summary:

As a Long-Term Care Consultant Pharmacist, I am dedicated to improving the quality of life for seniors through comprehensive medication management. By working closely with long-term care facilities and their residents, I can identify and resolve medication-related problems, optimize medication therapy, and improve adherence to prescribed regimens. Through my expertise in geriatric pharmacotherapy and patient counseling, I can provide seniors with the knowledge and skills they need to manage their medications effectively and achieve their health goals. Whether conducting medication reviews, counseling, or collaborating with other healthcare providers, I am committed to providing the highest level of care to my patients.

13- Hospital Pharmacist

Profile Headline: Hospital Pharmacist | Ensuring Safe and Effective Medication Use for Patients

Summary:
As a Hospital Pharmacist, I am dedicated to ensuring safe and effective patient medication use. By working closely with

healthcare providers, I can review medication orders, monitor drug therapy, and provide medication counseling to patients. Through my expertise in pharmacology and drug interactions, I am able to identify and resolve medication-related problems, optimize medication therapy, and improve patient outcomes. Whether preparing and dispensing medications, providing drug information to healthcare providers, or collaborating with other healthcare team members, I am committed to providing the highest level of care to my patients. With a passion for patient safety and a dedication to hospital pharmacy, I am proud to be a Hospital Pharmacist.

14- Community Pharmacist

Profile Headline: Community Pharmacist | Slaying Scripts | Improving Health Outcomes

Summary:

As a Community Pharmacist, I am committed to improving health outcomes and patient satisfaction one prescription at a time. By working closely with patients and healthcare providers, I am able to provide medication counseling, medication therapy management, and immunization services. Through my expertise in pharmacology and drug interactions, I am able to identify and resolve medication-related problems, optimize medication therapy, and improve patient outcomes. Whether it's providing medication education, collaborating with other members of the healthcare team, or offering health and wellness services, I am dedicated to providing the highest level of care to my patients.

15- Pharmacy Benefits Management Pharmacist

Profile Headline: Pharmacy Benefits Management Pharmacist | Maximizing Medication Value and Improving Patient Outcomes

Summary:

As a Pharmacy Benefits Management Pharmacist, I am dedicated to maximizing medication value and improving patient outcomes. By working closely with health plans, employers, and other stakeholders, I can develop and implement strategies to optimize medication use, reduce costs, and improve health outcomes. Through my expertise in pharmacoeconomics, formulary management, and medication utilization management, I am able to identify opportunities to improve medication therapy and reduce waste. Whether it's conducting drug utilization reviews, analyzing claims data, or collaborating with other members of the healthcare team, I am committed to providing the highest level of value-based care to my patients. With a passion for pharmacy benefits management and dedication to patient-centered care, I am proud to be a Pharmacy Benefits Management Pharmacist.

16- Drug Utilization Pharmacist

Profile Headline: Optimizing Medication Use and Improving Patient Outcomes

Summary:

As a Drug Utilization Pharmacist, I am dedicated to optimizing medication use and improving patient outcomes. By leveraging my expertise in pharmacotherapy, medication safety, and healthcare analytics, I am able to identify opportunities to improve medication therapy and reduce waste. Whether it's conducting drug utilization reviews, analyzing claims data, or collaborating with other members of the healthcare team, I am committed to providing the highest level of value-based care to my patients. Through my work in medication utilization management, I am able to develop and implement strategies to improve medication safety, reduce adverse drug events, and enhance patient satisfaction.

17- Pharmacy Supervisor of Pharmacy Manager

Profile Headline: Pharmacy Supervisor | Operations Management | Regulatory Compliance | Patient Care

Summary:

As a seasoned Pharmacy Supervisor, I have dedicated my career to ensuring the highest standards of quality, safety, and customer service in pharmacy operations. With extensive experience managing teams and overseeing day-to-day operations, I am committed to maintaining regulatory compliance and implementing best practices to enhance efficiency and productivity. My expertise in pharmacy operations management, inventory control, and patient care allows me to optimize workflows and streamline processes for optimal outcomes. As a skilled communicator and collaborator, I thrive in fast-paced environments and am adept at building solid relationships with colleagues, vendors, and patients alike. I am passionate about making a positive impact on patient health and safety through effective pharmacy management and leadership.

or

Summary:

As an experienced Pharmacy Manager, I have a proven track record of driving operational excellence, team development, and patient satisfaction. With a focus on optimizing workflow efficiencies, controlling inventory costs, and ensuring regulatory compliance, I have successfully led pharmacy teams to deliver exceptional care and service to patients. I am passionate about developing and mentoring staff to achieve their full potential, fostering a positive work culture, and implementing innovative strategies to improve patient care and satisfaction. Whether through implementing medication therapy management programs or collaborating with healthcare providers to enhance patient outcomes, I am committed to improving the quality of care and positively impacting patients' lives. With a deep understanding of pharmacy operations, industry trends, and emerging technologies, I am confident I can drive success in any healthcare setting.

18- Ambulatory Care Pharmacist

Profile Headline: Ambulatory Care Pharmacist | Optimizing Medication Therapy and Improving Patient Health

Summary:

As an Ambulatory Care Pharmacist, I am dedicated to optimizing medication therapy and improving patient health. By working closely with patients and healthcare providers in outpatient settings, I am able to provide medication counseling, medication therapy management, and disease state management services. Through my expertise in pharmacology and drug interactions, I am able to identify and resolve medication-related problems, optimize medication therapy, and improve patient outcomes. Whether it's providing medication education, collaborating with other members of the healthcare team, or offering health and wellness services, I am committed to providing the highest level of care to my patients.

19- Population Health Pharmacist

Profile Headline: Population Health Pharmacist | Advanced Practice | Direct Patient Care | Chronic Disease Management

Summary:

As an advanced practice Population Health Pharmacist, I am dedicated to improving patient outcomes in high-risk, high-cost, or complex populations in primary care settings. With specialized knowledge of pharmacotherapy and a passion for direct patient care, teaching, and consultation, I am committed to assuring optimal drug use outcomes and managing chronic disease states such as heart failure and diabetes. Through targeted interventions and measuring patient outcomes, I am able to drive measurable improvements in patient health and quality of life. As a skilled communicator and collaborator, I work closely with healthcare teams to develop comprehensive care plans and ensure seamless coordination of care. With a deep commitment to evidence-based practice, patient-centered care, and continuous improvement, I am confident that I can make a meaningful impact on population health and well-being.

20- Pharmacy Benefits Coordinator

Profile Headline: Pharmacy Benefits Coordinator | Medical Benefit Management | Specialty Drugs | Utilization Management

Summary:

As a Pharmacy Benefits Coordinator, I ensure optimal medical benefits and specialty drug management through clinical expertise and strategic interventions. With a deep understanding of drug therapy and utilization management, I am committed to maintaining and updating clinical criteria for drugs covered under the medical benefit and the managing site of care and white bagging programs to drive clinical and financial value. Through targeted interventions and engagement with providers and members, I can conduct meaningful interventions that improve pharmaceutical care and reduce the total cost of drug therapy. With a focus on evidence-based practice, patient-centered care, and cost-effective solutions, I am able to make a measurable impact on the health and well-being of our members while delivering tangible value to our organization.

21- Financial Planner

Profile Headline: Financial Planner | Wealth Management | Retirement Planning | Investment Strategies | Risk Management | Tax Planning

Summary:

As an experienced Financial Planner, I am dedicated to helping clients achieve their financial goals through effective wealth management, retirement planning, investment strategies, risk management, and tax planning. I have a proven track record of successfully developing and implementing personalized financial plans that maximize returns and minimize risks. I excel in conducting thorough economic analyses and utilizing the latest financial tools and technologies to deliver optimal results. I am passionate about staying up-to-date with the latest financial trends and regulations to ensure compliance and provide the best possible advice to clients. I am committed to building solid relationships with clients, understanding their unique needs and goals, and providing ongoing support and guidance throughout their financial journey.

22- Data Analyst

Profile Headline: Data Analyst | Data Visualization | Statistical Analysis | Data Modeling | Database Management | Business Intelligence

Summary:

As an experienced Data Analyst, I am dedicated to transforming raw data into actionable insights through data visualization, statistical analysis, data modeling, database management, and business intelligence. I have a proven track record of successfully analyzing complex data sets, identifying trends, and delivering strategic recommendations to drive business growth. I excel in developing and implementing data models, conducting thorough data analysis, and utilizing the latest data visualization tools to communicate insights to stakeholders effectively. I am passionate about leveraging the latest data management and analytics technologies for optimal results. I am committed to staying up-to-date with the latest data analytics trends and best practices to ensure the success of my projects and the organization—a Data Analyst who can transform raw data into actionable insights to drive business growth.

23- Entrepreneur

Profile Headline: Entrepreneur | Business Development | Strategic Planning | Marketing | Sales | Financial Management

Summary:

As an experienced Entrepreneur, I am dedicated to building and growing successful businesses through effective business development, strategic planning, marketing, sales, and financial management. I have a proven track record of successfully launching and scaling companies across various industries. I excel in identifying new business opportunities, developing and implementing practical business strategies, and building solid relationships with customers and stakeholders. I am passionate about leveraging the latest technologies and tools to drive business growth and innovation. I am committed to staying up to date with the latest business trends and best practices to ensure the success of my ventures.

24- Journalist

Profile Headline: Journalist | Investigative Reporting | Writing | Editing | Multimedia Storytelling | Interviewing

Summary:

I am dedicated to delivering high-quality news and information to audiences through investigative reporting, writing, editing, multimedia storytelling, and interviewing. I have a proven track record of producing impactful stories that inform and engage readers across various mediums. I excel in conducting thorough research and analysis to uncover newsworthy stories while adhering to the highest standards of journalistic ethics and integrity. I am passionate about using multimedia storytelling techniques, such as video, audio, and graphics, to enhance the impact of my reporting. I am committed to staying up to date with the latest trends and best practices in journalism to ensure the success of my stories and the publication.

25- Educator

Profile Headline: Educator | Curriculum Development | Instructional Design | Student Assessment | Classroom Management | Student Engagement

Summary:

An experienced teacher dedicated to delivering high-quality education and fostering a love of learning in students. My expertise lies in curriculum development, instructional design, student assessment, classroom management, and student engagement. I have a proven track record of successfully developing and implementing engaging and practical curriculum that meets the needs of diverse learners. I excel in creating dynamic and interactive learning environments that promote student engagement and foster creativity.

26- Operations Manager

Profile Headline: Operations Manager | Process Improvement | Supply Chain Management | Project Management | Quality Control | Cost Reduction

Summary:

Passionate about leveraging the latest technologies and tools to streamline operations and improve overall business performance. I am committed to staying up-to-date with the latest operations trends and best practices to ensure the success of my team and the organization. An experienced Operations Manager dedicated to optimizing business operations through process improvement, supply chain management, and project management. With expertise in quality control, cost reduction, and team leadership. I have a proven track record of successfully leading cross-functional teams to drive process improvements, reduce costs, and improve efficiency.

27- Sales Director

Profile Headline: Sales Director | Revenue Growth | Business Development | Sales Strategy | Sales Operations | Key Account Management

Summary:

As an experienced Sales Director, I am dedicated to driving revenue growth through effective business development and sales strategies. My expertise lies in sales strategy, sales operations, key account management, and team leadership. I have a proven track record of successfully building and leading high-performance sales teams while developing and implementing strategies that drive sales growth. I excel in identifying new business opportunities, building and nurturing relationships with key clients, and developing effective sales processes. I am passionate about leveraging the latest sales tools and technologies to drive sales productivity and improve customer engagement. I am committed to staying up to date with the latest sales trends and best practices to ensure the success of my team and the organization. If you are looking for a Sales Director who can drive revenue growth through effective business development and sales strategies, I am ready to help.

28- Marketing Director

Profile Headline: Marketing Director | Strategic Planning | Brand Management | Digital Marketing | Lead Generation | Marketing Analytics

Summary:

As an experienced Marketing Director, I am dedicated to developing and implementing effective marketing strategies that drive business growth. My expertise lies in strategic planning, brand management, digital marketing, lead generation, and marketing analytics. I have a proven track record of successfully launching and managing marketing campaigns that increase brand awareness and drive customer engagement. I am passionate about leveraging the latest marketing tools and technologies to deliver optimal results. I excel in cross-functional collaboration, working closely with sales, product development, and customer support teams to align marketing initiatives with business goals. I am committed to staying up to date with the latest marketing trends and best practices to ensure the success of my campaigns.

29- Human Resource Recruiter

Profile Headline: Human Resource Recruiter | Talent Acquisition | Employee Relations | Performance Management | Diversity and Inclusion | HR Compliance

Summary:

As an experienced Human Resource Recruiter, I am dedicated to sourcing and hiring top talent while building positive employee relations. My expertise lies in talent acquisition, performance management, diversity and inclusion, and HR compliance. I have a proven track record of successfully identifying and recruiting candidates for various roles across different industries. I am passionate about creating a positive employee experience and fostering a culture of inclusion and collaboration. I am committed to staying up-to-date with the latest HR trends and best practices to ensure compliance with employment laws and regulations. If you are looking for a Human Resource Recruiter dedicated to finding the best talent for your organization while fostering a positive and inclusive work environment, look no further.

30- IT Specialist

Profile Headline: Experienced IT Specialist | System Administration | Network Engineering | Software Development | Technical Support | Project Management

Summary:

As an experienced IT Specialist with a passion for technology, I have honed my skills in system administration, network engineering, and software development. With a proven track record of providing innovative solutions, I am committed to helping businesses optimize their technology systems and workflows. I excel in technical support and project management, with a keen eye for identifying opportunities for process improvement. I am dedicated to continued learning and development, staying up to date with the latest advancements in the field of IT. Whether working with small startups or large corporations, I am dedicated to building strong relationships with clients and colleagues alike.

Highlights of the Experience Section.

The experience section in most profiles reads exactly like a person's resume. Here are some tips to enhance this section:

Use the company icons.

If your experience includes companies with profiles on LinkedIn, choose the suggested auto-populated for your heading.

For example, if you worked for Apple Computers when you enter the company name, LinkedIn will suggest Apple, Computers & Manufacturing.

It is best to utilize the advised company instead of continuing to freehand. Now Apple Corporations icon will be displayed next to your experience and be a clickable hyperlink to the company's profile.

Why is this important? Not only does it provide a visual symbol recognizable to many, but it frees you from needing to explain what the company does in your description, thanks to the hyperlink and icon. Now you can focus the description of your job duties on your unique experience and skills acquired from the setting.

If you have your own business, this approach also applies. Create a profile for your business and ensure the profile picture is your logo. When listing your business in the experience section of your personal profile, the business logo will populate, and the link will lead to your business profile. This is a great opportunity to add another level of professionalism to your bio and drive traffic to your business!

Super special feature.

A key feature of the experience section is the ability to add media, videos, photos, or links. I highly suggest you take advantage of this little used gem of a feature to showcase publications and link to blogs or articles you have been referenced in, YouTube videos, or.

This is also a chance to give depth to your experience. The licenses and certifications section includes all certifications, including Masterclass, LinkedIn classes, and Coursera courses.

Make sure to list professional licenses in all states with active status.

Endorsements and Recommendations matter.

Others endorsing you is an important validation of your brand.

Choose the top 10 skills you want to showcase that fit well with your brand and are transferable for your next desired career choice.

One way to garner endorsements is to enforce others. Find the profile page of your colleagues, friends, and supervisors you know well and endorse the skills you believe are their true strengths. This typically generates a reciprocating action.

Recommendations carry more weight than endorsements and bring depth and social proof to your brand. Someone, who can be authenticated on LinkedIn, is expressing support with the weight of their professional reputation behind your brand.

Garnering this backing through requests or reciprocation is a huge step in validating your brand.

Summary.
Refresh your LinkedIn by blending in your personal brand.

Begin with your standout profile picture, working down through the page. Tell an authentic story that lets the reader learn who you are, where you've been, and what others say about you.

Compel them to want to know more.

Chapter Six

Real Estate Agent Example

SMART Goals:

- Increasing website traffic by 20% within six months, generating 50 new leads per month, or achieving a 15% increase in sales volume over the next quarter.

KPIs (Key Performance Indicators):

- KPIs: Number of leads generated, website traffic, social media engagement (likes, comments, shares), conversion rates (leads to clients), referrals, and sales volume.

Value-added statements:

- "Providing exceptional real estate experiences through personalized service, expert guidance, and in-depth market knowledge, helping you find your dream home and maximize your investment."

- "Delivering personalized service that exceeds expectations, ensuring your real estate goals are met with care and attention to detail."

- "Providing a seamless and stress-free experience by handling every aspect of your real estate journey, from initial consultation to closing, with professionalism and efficiency."

- "Going the extra mile to understand your unique needs and preferences, matching you with properties that align perfectly with your lifestyle, preferences, and investment goals."

Taglines:

- "Opening doors to new beginnings."

- "Your partner for life's biggest investments."

- "Simplifying your real estate journey, step by step."

- "Tailored solutions for your unique real estate needs."

- "Empowering you to make informed real estate decisions."

- "Bringing integrity and excellence to every transaction."

Instagram:

- Content ideas:

  Showcase visually appealing property photos and videos, behind-the-scenes footage of property tours,

  before-and-after transformation posts,

  client testimonials,

  local market updates.

- Hashtags:

#real estate agent, #dreamhome, #property for sale, #realestatephotography, #justlisted, #openhouse, #homebuying, #homesweethome.

- Collaboration:

Collaborate with local interior designers, home stagers, and mortgage lenders to cross-promote each other's services.

Twitter:

- Content ideas:

Post quick tips, real-time market updates, and relevant news articles, answer FAQs, and engage in conversations with followers.

- Hashtags:

#realestate, #propertynews, #housingmarket, #realtortips, #realestateadvice, #homebuying, #homeselling.

- Collaboration:

Partner with local businesses, such as moving companies or furniture stores, to offer exclusive discounts or joint promotions.

YouTube:

- Content ideas:

Create property tour videos, neighborhood guides, tutorials on home buying/selling processes, Q&A sessions, and virtual open houses.

- Collaboration:

Collaborate with local videographers, home inspectors, or contractors to provide valuable content and enhance your credibility.

Podcast:

- "Dream home."
- "Turning houses into homes, one sale at a time."
- "Real estate expertise you can rely on."
- "Where dreams become addresses."
- "Your key to a seamless real estate journey."
- "Making your real estate dreams a reality."
- "Guiding you home with passion and precision."
- "Your trusted advocate in the world of real estate."
- "Building relationships, one transaction at a time."
  - **Content ideas:** Discuss real estate trends, and investment strategies, interview local experts (e.g., mortgage brokers and real estate attorneys), and answer listener questions.
  - **Collaboration:** Invite other real estate agents, industry influencers, or professionals from related fields as guests on your podcast to diversify perspectives.

Facebook:

- Content ideas:

Share property listings, testimonials, local community events, homeowner tips, and educational blog posts.

- Hashtags:

  #realestateagent, #homesforsale, #propertylisting, #realestateexpert, #homeownership, #realestatetips.

- Collaboration:

  Partner with local photographers or home decor stores to provide engaging content and exclusive offers to your Facebook audience.

Pinterest:
- Content ideas:

  Create boards featuring interior design inspiration, home staging tips, DIY projects, local attractions, and market statistics.

- Hashtags:

  #homedecor, #realestateinspiration, #dreamhome, #realestateadvice, #homedesignideas, #homesellingtips.

- Collaboration:

  Collaborate with local bloggers or interior designers who curate content related to home improvement or lifestyle.

LinkedIn:
- Content ideas:

  Share industry insights, market trends, tips for first-time homebuyers/sellers, success stories, and articles showcasing your expertise.

- Hashtags:

#realestate, #realestateindustry, #housingmarket, #investmentproperty, #realtorlife, #realestateadvice.

- Collaboration:

  Connect with local professionals like lawyers, accountants, and contractors to provide comprehensive resources for clients.

  Headline: Experienced Real Estate Professional | Helping Clients Navigate the Path to Homeownership and Investment Success

About Section:

As an experienced real estate professional, I am dedicated to helping individuals and families achieve their homeownership and investment success dreams. With a strong background in the industry and a passion for providing exceptional service, I strive to make the real estate journey seamless and rewarding for my clients.

With in-depth knowledge of the local market, I am well-equipped to guide buyers and sellers through every step of the process. Whether you're a first-time homebuyer searching for the perfect starter home or a seasoned investor looking to expand your portfolio, I am committed to understanding your unique goals and tailoring my services to meet your needs.

I believe that open and transparent communication is key to building lasting relationships, and I pride myself on being a trusted advisor to my clients. I am here to provide guidance, answer questions, and address any concerns you may have throughout the entire transaction.

Utilizing the latest technology and innovative marketing strategies, I ensure your property receives maximum exposure to qualified buyers. For buyers, I employ a diligent approach to finding the right property, considering your budget, preferences, and long-term goals.

Beyond the transaction, I strive to be a valuable resource for my clients. Whether you need recommendations for trusted professionals, information on market trends, or assistance with post-purchase matters, I am here to provide ongoing support and guidance.

I invite you to connect with me to explore how I can assist you with your real estate needs. Together, we can navigate the exciting and ever-changing world of real estate, and I look forward to being your trusted partner on this journey.

Chapter Seven

―――――⌃―――――

Wedding Photographer Example

SMART Goals:

Booking at least 30 weddings in the next year, increasing social media engagement by 20% within six months, achieving a 90% client satisfaction rate, or growing revenue by 15% year-over-year.

KPIs (Key Performance Indicators):

KPIs: Number of inquiries generated, bookings, client satisfaction ratings, referral rates, social media engagement (likes, comments, shares), website traffic, and revenue growth.

Value-Added Statement:

"Capturing the Essence of Your Love Story: With a keen eye for detail and a passion for storytelling, I specialize in immortalizing the precious moments of your wedding day. By blending a photojournalistic approach with artistic creativity, I aim to deliver timeless images that beautifully reflect the emotions, joy, and intimacy of your special day."

Taglines:

- "Preserving Love, One Frame at a Time."

- "Crafting Timeless Memories of Your Perfect Day."

- "Capturing the Moments, Embracing the Love."

- "Transforming Love Stories into Art."

- "Relive Your Wedding Day, Forever."

Instagram:

- Content ideas:

  Showcase stunning wedding photos, and behind-the-scenes shots, highlight real wedding stories, share wedding tips and inspiration, and feature client testimonials.

- Hashtags:

  #weddingphotographer, #brideandgroom, #weddinginspiration, #weddingday, #bridetobe, #loveandmarriage, #weddingdetails.

- Collaboration:

  Collaborate with wedding planners, bridal boutiques, makeup artists, and florists to cross-promote each other's services.

Twitter:

- Content ideas:

  Post sneak peeks of recent weddings, share quick wedding photography tips, engage in conversations with couples planning their big day, and share blog posts about wedding photography.

- Hashtags:

  #weddingphotography, #weddingmoments, #weddinginspo, #bridalphotographer, #weddingtips, #ido, #weddingphotographyideas.

- Collaboration:

  Collaborate with wedding bloggers, bridal magazines, and wedding-related vendors to create joint content and promotions.

YouTube:
- Content ideas:

  Create behind-the-scenes videos of wedding shoots, tutorials on posing and composition, client testimonials, highlight reels of real weddings, and advice for couples on choosing a wedding photographer.

- Collaboration:

  Collaborate with wedding planners, videographers, and makeup artists to create comprehensive wedding-related content and provide a well-rounded perspective.

Podcast:
- Content ideas:

  Discuss wedding photography trends, interview brides, grooms, and industry experts, share stories and insights from memorable weddings, and offer tips for capturing beautiful wedding moments.

- Collaboration:

  Invite wedding planners, florists, and other wedding vendors as guests on your podcast to provide a holistic view of the wedding industry and foster cross-promotion.

Facebook:
- Content ideas:

  Share photo albums of recent weddings, client testimonials, wedding planning tips, industry news, and blog posts on wedding photography topics.

- Hashtags:

  #weddingphotography, #weddingmoments, #weddingphotographer, #weddinginspiration, #bridetobe, #happilyeverafter.

- Collaboration:

  Partner with wedding venues, DJs, and rental companies to offer exclusive packages or discounts for engaged couples.

Pinterest:
- Content ideas:

  Create boards featuring wedding photography inspiration, bridal portrait ideas, wedding photo poses, wedding album design inspiration, and tips for capturing candid moments.

- Hashtags:

  #weddingphotography, #bridalinspiration, #weddingposes, #weddingphotoideas, #weddingphotographytips, #bridesofpinterest.

- Collaboration:

  Collaborate with wedding bloggers and event designers to curate visually appealing boards and collaborate on styled shoots.

LinkedIn:

- Content ideas:

  Share professional wedding photography insights, industry trends, personal experiences capturing weddings, and valuable tips for engaged couples.

- Hashtags:

  #weddingphotography, #weddingindustry, #bridalphotography, #weddingseason, #weddingphotographerlife, #weddingphotographytips.

- Collaboration:

  Connect with wedding venues, event coordinators, and caterers to build referral networks and offer comprehensive wedding packages.

LinkedIn Headline:

Exquisite Wedding Photographer | Capturing Timeless Moments of Love | Preserving Memories to Last a Lifetime

LinkedIn About Section:

As a passionate wedding photographer, I specialize in capturing the beauty, emotion, and magic of one of life's most significant milestones. With an artistic eye and a dedication to storytelling, I strive to create breathtaking images that not only freeze moments in time but also evoke the genuine emotions and unique essence of each couple's love story.

With years of experience in the wedding industry, I understand the importance of delivering exceptional service and creating a seamless experience for my clients. From the initial consultation to the final delivery of their treasured photographs, I am committed to providing personalized attention, understanding their vision, and exceeding their expectations.

I believe that wedding photography is not just about taking pictures but about crafting a visual narrative that encapsulates the joy, romance, and profound connections shared on such a special day. I pour my heart and soul into each image, aiming to create timeless artwork that couples will proudly display and cherish for generations to come.

Collaboration is at the core of my work, and I enjoy partnering with wedding planners, venues, and other industry professionals to bring dream weddings to life. Together, we ensure that every detail is flawlessly captured, reflecting each couple's unique personalities and styles.

I invite you to explore my portfolio and witness the stories I have had the privilege to tell through my lens. If you're seeking a dedicated and talented wedding photographer who understands the significance of this once-in-a-lifetime event, I would be honored to be a part of your journey. Let's connect and discuss how I can help you preserve your most cherished memories in breathtaking photographs.

Conclusion

Several years ago, I created an Instagram page that was a fun, personal journey at the time. Though it was "public," I did not use my name and didn't invite anyone I knew to follow the page. I wanted to blend into the worldwide sea of anonymity, escaping my small-town life. The page began with zero followers. I posted twice a week, at 5 a.m., before I started getting ready for the day. The posts would include hashtags related to the picture, and the caption would consistently be a song lyric I felt coordinated with the featured pic. The tone of the post was my authentic voice; I thoughtfully and kindly replied to any comments. After two years, the Instagram account had grown from 0 followers to 16,000.

If my account with goofy selfies, song lyrics, and a couple of hashtags can organically grow without a marketing team, ads, or professional equipment, you my friend, can do amazing with a plan, some time, and consistent effort.

A good social media posting strategy involves planning, consistency, and engagement. Here are some key steps to create a solid social media posting strategy:

Set your goals. Determine what you want to achieve with your social media presence, such as increasing brand awareness, driving website traffic, or generating leads.

Knowing who your target audience is, understanding what kind of content they're interested in, monitoring which content creates the most engagement, and soliciting ideas for content from your audience.

Choose the right social media platforms that align with your goals and audience. For example, if your target audience is predominantly young, then platforms such as Snapchat and Instagram might be the best fit. If your audience is more professional, then LinkedIn might be the right platform for you.

Plan your content in advance by creating a content calendar. This will help you stay organized and consistent in your posting. Determine the frequency of your posts and the types of content you'll be sharing.

Optimize your content for each platform by using the appropriate formats, such as videos, images, or text posts. Use keywords and hashtags to help your content show up in search results.

Engaging with your audience is critical to building a loyal following and increasing your reach. Respond to comments and messages, participate in community conversations, and encourage your audience to share your content.

Monitor your social media metrics, such as engagement rate, follower growth, and website traffic, to determine the success of your posting strategy. Use this data to refine your strategy and improve your results over time.

Remember, building a large social media audience takes time and consistency. Focus on creating valuable content, engaging with your audience, and continually refining your strategy. Stay authentic and committed to providing value, and your audience will grow over time.

Made in the USA
Columbia, SC
07 February 2024

31664798R00061